DEITY-ALPHABETS

———————

poems

*Mike and Ann
with much
affection.
Carroll*

DEITY-ALPHABETS

poems

Carroll C. Kearley

TEBOT BACH • HUNTINGTON BEACH • CALIFORNIA • 2009

Cover image: UCLA Charles E. Young Research Library Department of
                 Special Collections, The Armenian Gospels of Gladzor
Design, layout: Melanie Matheson, Rolling Rhino Communications

ISBN 13: 978-1-893670-42-6
ISBN 10: 1-893670-42-2

Library of Congress Control Number: 2009932095

A Tebot Bach book

Tebot Bach, Welsh for little teapot, is A Nonprofit Public Benefit Corporation which sponsors workshops, forums, lectures, and publications. Tebot Bach books are distributed by Small Press Distribution, Armadillo, Ingram, and Bernhard De Boer.

The Tebot Bach Mission: Advancing Literacy, Strengthening Community, and transforming life experiences with the power of poetry through readings, workshops, and publicatons.

This book is made possible by a grant from The San Diego Foundation Steven R. and Lera B. Smith Fund at the recommendation of Lera Smith.

www.tebotbach.org

For those homeless people on Arizona Avenue who have been the inspiration for these poems, and for my wife Tacui Tatiana, Judy "Black Boots" Coleman, my sons Chris and Greg, my grandson Nick and my granddaughter Lauren Tatiana.

I must acknowledge the critical guidance I received from David St. John and the poets I met in his extraordinary workshops at the Ruskin Art Club. A special thank you goes to Elena Karina Byrne, my editor and mentor, to Mifanwy Kaiser, my publisher, Tebot Bach, and to those people who graciously supported me as I brought this collection into being.

CONTENTS

T JOINTS AND BUTTERFLIES

NOWHERE'S NOWHERE

ALPHABETS, END TO END

INTRODUCTION

PAINTING THE SOUL
by Garry Wills

Carroll Kearley has spent years stopping by an outdoor market in Santa Monica where homeless men and women gather to beg, sell, or entertain. He does not go there to understand or report on their "plight." His aim is not that of a sociologist or journalist or documentarian. He is just interested in them as people, each with distinctive tastes and a personal story. He uses his poetry to get inside the individuals and voice their inner selves. It is a labor of love and admiration. The poems voice not only dreams deferred or hopes broken, but tiny victories, affordable vanities, and survival strategies. We meet some people who fight bravely for dignity, or some who are giving up the fight:

> These are not streets for the faltering
> who cannot keep the course for the day
> or follow shadow-rhythms into night.

There are no "types" here, only individuals whose traits Kearley cherishes for their own sake. He is like a Goya who comes to paint the soul.

These are people who sing, who mock each other, protect each other, bluff or bully or outwit their poet-observer. We meet and like them with him:

> Dave's body is choreographed by cerebral palsy.
> He tried to make me understand more than his name.
> His body twists in the wheelchair as I bend
> to unravel threads of tortured talk.

There is the man who served time for armed robbery:

> Boring labor in prison weakened his wrath,
> made him a Bible reader, forced him to pray.

Some perform little services for tips:

> His days as merchant marine long gone,
> Johnie's a photo negative of Abraham Lincoln—
> tall, bony, black, with a white beard.
> Sundays, he takes care of dogs and bikes
> while people eat and shop in their leisurely way.

Others guard their few possessions:

> A lover more dear than any other,
> grade-A ex spent his money to pull
> her back from riptide drugs. Undercurrents
> pulled her down, alone, to set up home
> on grimy streets. In a grocery cart
> she pushed beer cans, clothes, a sleeping bag.

Some boast of their ability to live on the street, shunning the shelters with "cruel rules." Kearley wanders through his gallery of the gritty and the grave, getting to know them ever better, winning their trust, sharing their jokes.

> Marks of their individual grace amaze me. ❧

PREFATORY REMARKS

T here was no plan. *Meeting the homeless* was not on my agenda. It came about by happenchance. Some thirty years ago, on Wednesdays, I started to visit Arizona Avenue's outdoor market. For several years I kept walking by the homeless, sometimes giving a dollar bill or two. One day I stopped to talk with Cynthia and Jerry. They were sitting on the sidewalk, under the "No Parking" sign next to the vehicular entrance to the Post Office on Arizona Avenue in Santa Monica. Cynthia's witty chirp and Jerry's sub-servient docility intrigued me. Soon I was talking to them every week. To be exact, Cynthia and I did most of the talking. Later, when they went their separate ways, Jerry began to talk to me in a confidential manner.

I met Bo J. He was so polite and sang songs, mainly blues, beautiful to my ear and mind. He was always at the edge of the crowd's activity. He is a loner, who likes to sing for an individual or a small group, quietly, with feeling in his voice.

Nameless, at first, did not want to converse with me. Maybe some pro-found hurt reduced her to silence. She wanted her sign BROKE AND THAT'S NO JOKE to talk for her. When she finally agreed to share talk, she became vocal, revealing an intelligent wit. Her mind is quick, precise. I haven't seen her for several years.

Then there was Sos, without hands, flitting in the crowd of buyers. I began to talk to her, not for long, for she was always on the move. Her friend Tom told me most of what I know about her. He became her protector after she was raped.

Marie tells her story, a larger one full of small ones. She likes to shock. "They kicked me out of my free apartment, because I kept on smoking." "My son's coming out here for Christmas. He's a real redneck."

When I first started to talk with Johnie, I caught on quickly that he was a man who relished bantering. He was guardian of dogs and bicycles for busy shoppers. He could, and can, outtalk me any day. I am more meditative than verbal.

After establishing these friendly bonds, I wanted to lend my voice to these homeless people to help them to tell their stories. But I was neither poet, nor journalist, nor novelist, nor sociologist.

A catalytic event turned me into a minor poet. My mother died. I felt the only way to express my feelings about her was to write a poem. I wrote the poem. A cataract broke loose in me. Six hundred poems about many things followed. I was an auto-didact in the art of poetry, with all the deficiencies thereof. ❧

❧ BOUQUET

I absorb sensibility from this poet
who had to bear more…
        and to her, in return

I bring most common flowers,
buttercups and pink carnations,
should she come alive in a breath,
confidant, to walk with me today,

Gabriela Mistral, Chilean poet,
Nobel Prize winner when I was young,
never married, never bore a child,
nurtured motherhoods with lullabies.
The partridge sleeps in the clover
listening to the beat of its heart.
Her dearest friend and her adopted son
took their own lives.   Devastation.
             Desolation
The wind like a scythe slashes.

Teacher, whose formal education ended
at eleven, she stands at the door
of the country school near La Serena,
watching her children coming barefoot,
cuts and bruises, precious feet,
raising clouds of dust, patient steps.

Tenderness. Her life was a plea
for little ones not flesh of her flesh,
and she brought forth poems as a mother
brings a child out of the blood of her heart,
each poem a *copihue* blossom,
"most beautiful climber in the world."

bell-like, deep red, national flower,
a "wept tear" for Mapuche Indian dead,

and her presence appears
here on this street, where
I have walked many years,
and each homeless person
I converse with once was a child.

WHERE WAST THOU?

❧ ALPHABETS

A project,
fanciful, not realistic,
of serious intent, is insistent,
almost personally: these homeless people
who sleep in odd places
and ask for money on market day—
let's make their names known.

Consider how Jasper Johns
used numbers and words
like *blue* and *red* as motifs
when he painted *Zero Through Nine*,

how Paul Klee,
filling *Southern Gardens*
and *Fire at Full Moon*
with tapestries of colored polygons,
used optics of light
to create rhythm and mood,

how Ben Shahn's trombones, thick hands,
masks and webs of crisscross lines came to
Cat's Cradle in Blue, *Goyescas*, and *Chicago*,

and consider how he linked the letterpress era
and twenty-two letters from the Hebrew alphabet
to design his orange chop, that Japanese seal stone
for personal signature, used in his last years
to stamp his identity whenever...and so,

why not
ask a compositor
to take pieces of cast metal type,
each a letter from the alphabet,
to form the first name and last

of each homeless person,
then, using many colors of ink,
print them on pastel paper,
over and over again, handouts,
to proclaim that each bearer of a name
has an irreplaceable impress?

❧ ASKING FAVORS

Live with an artist long enough,
and you can start asking favors.

No matter if Rembrandt van Rijn
is three hundred twenty-four years older than I.
When I walk Arizona Avenue on market day,
he joins me, at my elbow, a spiritual friend,
to chat with overrun and under-sung
women and men, who once had a bed at home,
in better days or worse, but don't anymore.

His etchings focus on details:
houses with thatched roofs…
an aging man making water, frontal view,
weathered, big-belly beggarly,
everything wrapped in a bundle on his back,
his cap like a sunken loaf of bread…
landscapes stretching far…an old woman,
bent, a basket on her arm, burdened,
talking to a concerned younger man,
hunched, too, leaning on his walking stick…
lines on elderly faces, dress-up vanities…
how he loved elegant hats for self-portraits,
like towers or pillows… speaking of pillows,
the canopied bed, light shining
on the young man's tenderness,
pants still on, love aglow, her head
pillowed, face blissful, together even now,
Adam and Eve all over again.

Musicians perform, absolutely poor,
at the half-swinging door,
worn faces inside the house and without…
Jesus alive in etchings repeatedly
from glowing birth to end-stopped maturity,

unpretending hands and eyes,
all the Bach-like keys of kind discernment,
his eyes empowered by Rembrandt's own,
lending mine focus for care
to observe people gathered on this street
and those who pause in graphic art,
like the beggar with his peg leg forever.

❧ DOUBLE WILLARD

Both faces, synchronized, concentrate,
fingers touching their eyelids and brows
above lips intent to enunciate.

> "Learn from this pain here.
> You will never feel it again."

In front of a plate-glass window
at the Discovery Channel store,
Willard and his double, unkempt,
wear identical clothes, no shirt,
a vest, baggy pants, scarf round the neck,
flipped back, each
a player on his stage…

walk, turn, consider,
react to his own image,

exhorting that other self,

two earnest mouths,
dialogue in unison,
never to forget lessons that count hurt…

two strangely clad orators gesticulate,
urge action to succeed, plead…

some casually curious onlookers
            intrude, break
Double-Willard's performance…

the vest, the chest in the mirror
disappearing, almost on fire
with light from the descending sun.

❧ HEMEROCALLIS

The flowers of most species
open at sunrise and wither
at sunset....
      —*Wikipedia*

Willard like a scruffy daylily
blooms and withers.
There are days he sleeps a lot, here
on the Promenade, head cradled
on a Tempur-Pedic curbstone.
He sleeps where crowds walk, as if
demonstrating concentration, as if
acting a part with professional skill,
one of the world's great sleepers,
someone who can lock us out
even when we walk inches from his head.

How can one who sleeps like this
unfurl to be a human plant, all arms,
waving branches, doubling himself
in show windows, reaching out in speech
like an unfolding, a blossoming
member of a species we prize
from the garden of oratory?

🍂 MIRROR-ME-PERFORMANCE

Shoes smashed down at the heels
and worn like old slippers,
I suggest, need replacing.

 Willard says,
"Shoes are not important."

His intense dramatic show
could go on were he barefoot
or were he dressed in clothes
from Saks Fifth Avenue.
His rhetorical skills double
in the showcase window
to challenge the man confronting him.
Like a painter of graffiti in high gear,
five brushes in each hand,
he waves his arms to impress
his convictions on reflective glass
in all the emotional colors of affirmation
found in a box of colored Pentel pens.

Or,
like a concert pianist
performing on the street, his keyboard
the familiar figure mirrored in glass,
he plays his own cacophonous concerto
with voices of outdoor-market buyers
as volunteer orchestra. His left arm rises,
his hand then, in full descent, fingers curled,
strikes chord after chord, while
his flying, gesticulating right arm
directs its hand in sweeping runs
of discordant homeless melodies.

Until,
even the casual observer
feels fatigue from watching
this persistent performer
demonstrate his art without concern
for passing time
and never ask for pay.

❧ TRAMPLED GARDENS

Is it too much to ask
three aging guitarists
with arthritic fingers
to play tango rhythms for me
while I sing in trembling voice?

I dwell by happenstance
on the homeless
who feel and sleep the streets.
Filthy hands. Some drug-depressed,
bipolar, just lost. Dirty clothes.
Don't try to explain.
Wind-lost butterflies,
blown wingless like leaves.
Hummingbirds of humor glow.
Crows and gulls look for food.
Noble all the way to mean.
Hurt to the bone. *Don't cry for me.*
Broken thistles. Trampled gardens.
Columbines fade. Delphiniums, too.
Tomato vines turn brown.
Where will we be tomorrow?

❧ FAR AWAY AND NEAR AT HAND

In this Republic of Santa Monica,
chronically homeless people
settle to stay, well, stay for a while.
Thirty years I have watched them
taking part, so to speak, in a film
No House Number for Me, neorealism,
actors non-professional, documentary style,
unscripted, simple events, episodic structure,
struggle, pathos and comedy, compassion,
like *Bicycle Thieves* and *Open City*.

Worldwide, markets are magnets,
            drawing crowds
to sell, buy, share,
            and to hear music from the air.
Neighborhoods come alive.

The poor collect where ordinary people
are apt to give a bit, then listen.
"I have a story," each broke person
might say, "a mix of personal twists
worth a laugh and a cry.
Can you spare some time?"

Here in Santa Monica, Wednesdays,
            Arizona Avenue, Second to Sixth,
people mill about, buying from stands,
            talking, hastening, hearing

Bolivian woodwinds haunt highlands,
Mexican guitarists, striking strings, singing
solo, while Tommy Joe intones the blues
with seventh chords, dominant and diminished,
echoing moods of melancholy and depression.

Medleys of song celebrate the human mix.
Pay to rhythm! Strong beats and weak! Clap, clap!
Join the chorus! Clap, clap!

❧ TWO BREATHS

Tom's courtly-clean on Arizona Avenue.
Homeless panhandle here, outdoor market day,
midweek smell, most clothes throwaways,
but Tom does laundry every week.

Now Sos—
rhyme it with *close* (to whom?)
or *dose* of misfortune—
she does not have hands,
just a small thumb, oddly placed, adept,
on her left arm stub, a clasp to hold bills.

She's forty-five.
Tom's the knight who guards her since the rape.
Petite Thalidomide-orphan, Sos darts
among those who buy vegetables and flowers,
gathering her sympathy-money faster than most.
Tom's embarrassment at being here to plead
fosters hesitation, curtails income.

Sos dared to say, "We could rent a room
just for the night. We could take showers.
We could sleep in a motel bed, you and me,
each on the proper side. I'll pay the way."

Sometimes they camp on the sand nearby,
below Ocean Park, a frugal holiday,
a pup-tent for each. Sos empties
her all-purpose bag on a towel,
then uses toes to organize her things,
like a handicapped street vendor
laying out wares, or like my mother
emptying her purse on the marriage bed
on a February day when sheets
in rural Idaho froze white on the clothesline,

and she had to start somewhere
to put order in a farmhouse that never knew
the rule *everything has its place.*

Tom does not urge intimacy. He recognizes
their mutual need to stay two breaths away.

❧ HAMMERED DOWN

Outside the Post Office, cement benches collect homeless,
mainly men, to exchange half-reckless, contradicting views.
When a woman joins, they encourage her to play the sparring games.

"You looking for the guy who did the deed?"

"I couldn't take the beatings any more
when he was drunk. Here I am, alone.
Pregnant, you see. I know he loves me,
halfway. I feel the same. But no more,
and I don't know how or anything else."

"You thought about this, enough?"

"Should I go back? He always says he'll try.
I was drinking, too. More than a tad."

"Pauline, a kid belongs with his dad."

"I don't know what the baby will be.
You guys just think it's got to be a boy,
if, in your fat eyes, it's going to count."

"You can't raise a kid here. Crazy!"

"It's part of me now.... For good."

"I saw your picture in the *LA Times*,
a celebrity, famous for poverty and pregnancy,
sleeping in an empty building, downtown.
Why're you here?"

Taking hold of her canvas bag,
placing it firmly on her lap,
Pauline starts to explain her life,

earnestly, like a sixth-grade teacher
introducing a case in social studies.

"I don't have a center anymore.
I'm scared all the time. You guys don't know
what my life is like, under all the blows,
like a house hammered down, hammered apart.
I don't know where to go."

❧ A SPARROW'S WORTH

Sparrows have fallen from higher estates,
their social evolution spinning in reverse.
Passer domesticus, our House Sparrow,
copulates indecently worldwide.

Hen and cock wear the ash-blue crown.
Their other clothes look like those
selected in Salvation Army stores
or found in thrift stores for the blind.

Gulls and crows do not respect
sparrows' manners when they eat.
The bigger birds scare smaller ones
from morsels scattered near the market stand.

Sydney and Dianne are cock and hen.
Seated in his wheelchair among the shoppers,
Sydney keeps an eye on his dark bipolar love
perched on the three-foot wall in front of the bank.

Matthew could have had Jesus say, "See
those birds in the sky. The Father feeds them all.
Not one sparrow pecks at weed or flower seed
without His eyes measuring bird-deep worth."

Dave's body is choreographed by cerebral palsy.
He tries to make me understand more than his name.
His body twists in the wheelchair as I bend
to unravel threads of tortured talk.

❧ SO IT GOES

"She's fake and you're fricken dumb
to help her dull her mind with drugs."
The SUV driver, approaching the light,
fired away. What to reply? Should I say
it's false, my lady, to have a frozen heart?

Ellen stepped into the street, held up
her actress' hands, delivered words,
dramatizing misfortune's
intrepid panhandling art.

The pilot of power and integrity
turned left, leaving us subdued.

These are not streets for the faltering
who cannot keep the course for the day
or follow shadow-rhythms into night.

The homeless sleep, blanketed cocoons.
Come morning, these evanescent poor
do chores, folding sleeping bags,
making beds in houses cruel with rules.
They come. They go. Their beg-a-likes
are not alike. They work the streets.
Their word is *work*. Try it for fun!

Several visit Starbucks, six until noon,
knowing dollars come to the door.
This fellow hopes to unpack crates
at a stand selling rainbow-colored cauliflower
along with red, white, and blue potatoes.

"The work or me, which one won't last?'"
And so it goes. Any mix to calm the pangs
and quell the cravings. There's no quitting now.
"We have to meet the day's demands."

❧ ALETHEA

She has been style queen among have-nots here:
a blue-and-white polka-dot dress, fifties' style,
reaching half way between ankles and knees,
purchased at St. Joseph's Thrift Shop,
accented with flaming lipstick
and a red beret atop bleached blond hair.
I listen to her speak through herself to me.

"Alethea, I ask myself under my breath,
why has your beauty gone for good?
My sweet manner has not protected me
from a spiraling down from starting low.
Arizona Avenue, my daytime home,
must serve as crowded living room.
At night I sleep away from friends,
charity bed (beware of men, Mother said!).

"She ran Alpha Home in Houston.
You can't forget where you came from
or where you're trying to go, heaven bound
for me, I hope. In the end I'm sure to know.
She took in broken women from prison
and women like me, fragile from alcohol.
They marveled at my beauty, sweet docility
not earned by stringing out intentions.
Eighteen women, no men, formed a family,
First Gospel Church sponsored and financed.

"Born in Texas, I was a forty-nine baby girl.
Daddy was a sailor boy on ships in the War.
He could no more stay in one place than I,
before Worn-Out stamped a brand on me abruptly.

"Mother lived with vast ideals, ignoring him.
He could not break her New Testament dreams.

I was all right while she needed help,
and there I stayed until I closed her eyes,
younger than mine, milder, more profound.
She cried for help to love beyond her strength.
Her charity's lips were not sufficient defense
against cancer's brutality, pursuing me now."

❧ GIVE ME FOR STARTS ONE PART AT LEAST OF A GENEROUS SMILE.

This sign makes it personal, clear and direct
that Brooks, showing his hand, appeals.
At his Fourth and Santa Monica territorial spot
he strokes his beard, soliciting coins and bills.

"What brings you here to get a livelihood?"
"Thirty-five years in a stretch of prison time."
Time to think a lot, fading somewhat more
each afternoon when the key turned in the lock.

"I was", he says, "a runaway train.
My drunken engineer raced the tracks."
In Los Angeles he turned seven and sad
when Mother left him an orphan, scared.

California Youth Authority taught him
to grab when grabbing was good, and lose.
He found hours to hate and hours to wait
for the break to Colbert, Red River town.

He went to find his father's parents' place;
found no one there, felt hollow and wild,
drank with women, knew them at night.
Stayed on. Six year later he bought the gun.

The rampant man brings fear and shame to the town.
"Armed robbery gets you thirty-five years."
Boring labor in prison weakened his wrath,
made him a Bible reader, forced him to pray.

"Don't ever wannta go back. Never.
No room in the pen, freedom, women to love.
Bad people out there scare this old ram
who's more like a lamb wanting its mother's milk."

❧ SANTA SEVERINA

Severina, from Belize,
burnt-carmine-skinned pobrecita,
prayer-enclosed mendicant,
sits by the hour on a folding chair
behind a truck at the eastern end
of the outdoor market.

    "Dios le bendiga."
    "May God bless you."

Her thanks for coins and bills.
No sign. No verbal request.
No hand held out.
Only a rosary to ask for help.
She's a miniature, tranquility-built,
holy-medal shrine in a secular place.

Did she once dance with fiery steps,
banter with dozens of would-be lovers,
watch the door, wait at night
for the one to come?

Did she learn in personal despair
the air suggesting *Santa Severina?*
Is she other than what she seems?
How about any of us?

    "Dios le bendiga."

🙠 FRIENDLY ACQUAINTANCES

who ask for money
on this street, hopefully

André is Zapotec, from Oaxaca.
"I'm fine," is his refrain.

Diabetes took his left leg
in life's high-stake game.

"Dialysis three times a week
keeps my kidneys ready to go."

Tremors and quivers
of rapture and worry
trek to the surface
of each street-worn face,
serving as signs
soliciting help.

Chris, with bone-claw arthritic hands,
collects coins and bills in a coffee can,
to pay his way back to Hong Kong
to teach English in school, giving advice

such as he offers me:

"Please don't eat sour.
Oranges not good for you.
Not good for stomach and bathroom."

MARKET DAY

His days as merchant marine long gone,
Johnie's a photo negative of Abraham Lincoln:
tall, bony, black, with a white beard.
Sundays, he takes care of dogs and bikes
while people eat and shop in their leisurely way.
Today, he flings second-hand wit at those passing by,
improvising like a deckhand on a boring day at sea.
"Hey, Handsome Man, I've been looking for you.
Where's that grey felt hat that sets your style?"
He doesn't hesitate to ask, "Hey, Beautiful Lady,
could you set me up for a cup of coffee, even lunch?"

Farm people leave sleep at three or four
to truck home-grown produce into the city.
Driving miles before dawn to continue work,
half are apt to say, "How could anyone choose
to sleep on the street like a stray dog or alley cat,
and during the day pester shoppers for a buck?"

In the market's crowd it's look, move, dodge, pause,
sidestep, bump, maybe say, "Excuse me,"
then stop to buy at multicolored stands: piles
of tomatoes, asparagus, oranges, artichokes,
radicchio, lettuce, eggplant, cauliflower. Now

Marie was far from the prettiest girl in school.
She married an abusive, lecherous proto-rat,
soon ran away from him to come west alone.
At sixty she lives in an ancient VW van, parks
for the night behind Liberty Income Service, becoming
a caterpillar-dream, wearing the familiar white canvas hat,
billowing, prevailing in the sea-van as she turns
into a butterfly with sunflower-yellow and sea-green wings.

Wednesdays, for five hours, she stands politely alert
here at Arizona and Third, her money cup ready.

"When I got back to my van yesterday,
it was like a ransacked house, but it was me,
you know what I mean, a violation.
They tossed everything every which way
until they found my little bucket of money."

❧ INVITATION TO GEORGE SEGAL, SCULPTOR

Segal always comes off
as the humanist of pop art.
—John Haber

No reason at all not to ask.
He only died recently, not long
after finishing "Breadline,"
"Fireside Chat," "The Rural Couple,"
in bronze, Room 2, FDR Memorial.
Remember, also, those white plaster figures,
almost ghostly, ordinary people,
like the two men standing in serious talk,
and that young couple nearby, close,
on a bench in Sheridan Square.

Segal could memorialize
my homeless acquaintances
in melancholic white plaster.
Cynthia for sure. Let her wear
her dirty baseball cap
and a long pink coat,
hands sun-and-wind-blown raw.

Segal understood
what plaster-impregnated bandages
could do for sculpture. Apply water, blow-dry
the enshrining cast, cut it, knife-knowing, deft.
Cynthia's greased face, hands, clothes wouldn't stick.
Details I'll leave aside for now, but
I would definitely like a resurrected Segal
to do a dozen of these men and women
to sit or stand permanently along this street,
between Second and Sixth,
hands held out.

THE CAMP

🐦 DESOLATE SPARROW

Street ways control.

Her beauty should be beauty of the Anna's Hummingbird:
metallic green, freckled breast, the garden's moving jewel,
        columbine aerialist.
Not so. It surely was way back when, but it won't be
ever again. Tarnished face, no glamorous glow.

Every winter a soiled pink coat covers cracked knees.
Dirt accumulates dark under nails, sweat-stained cap
        crown for this queen.

A staph infection (clinic-treated) leaves open sores
on dirt-caked fingers, the backs of her hands. She feels sick.
Sits under a NO PARKING sign. Vomits her food.
"The antibiotic, dosage must change."

Jerry, sweet man now for a long while, is, she says,
on the lonesome bitter crack road. "We've been together
a while, but we're not a pair." Mario, contesting,
has gone for beer. He's jealous. "Stay away from her!"
She's been to rehab a decade ago, and doesn't do drugs.
Unless she lies. But, god, how she needs money for beer.

Mario keeps a gun under permit. Unless he lies.
"I'll shoot him when he touches you again."
Jerry wants the feel of her hands at night.
Twenty years back, a high school kid,
he sold produce from the back of his dad's truck.

"Better not. You'll go to jail." Cynthia confuses her role
in the triangular drama played round the clock
on a four-block Arizona Avenue urine-acrid stage.

Sometimes she prays. Prays for Jerry.
She still has a vintage store of impertinent chirps.
We talk a while. I give her a bill. "God bless," she says.

❧ IF NO ONE SHIRKS

Behind establishments
going east and south
from the bar called West End,
in the open rectangular space
the Camp takes form at dusk.
Owners have grumbled, "Okay.
We can use security guards. Clean up.
Out by seven. No trouble"

The Camp has rules: up by six,
litter collected, tossed, sleeping bag
or mattress stashed. No mess.
Serves four adequately, if no one shirks.
As for comfort, better for two.
Often five or six collect. In winter rain,
like a litter of puppies at their mother's dugs,
they line up under the only overhang.

Cynthia and Jerry, a pair pro tem,
rule the Camp, setting rules begrudgingly
to keep from being asked to leave.
Cynthia stirs early, groggy from beer and sleep,
self-appointed director, a smudged pink coat
falling in well-worn cascades to her ankles.
She does take charge, issuing commands,
if she has not been with Mario for the night.

Her baseball cap pulled down emphatically,
she asserts, "Those two have to go.
A dog, two wheelchairs, sloppy ways.
We sympathize to a point. I'm tired
of enforcing with my tongue.
Would you want to share a home
with two not-so-very-nice people?
They fake nine-tenths of their disabilities."

❧ BOTTLEBRUSH TREE

I was not born to sleep beneath the bottlebrush tree.
My parents rose at dawn to work
until no strength stayed in muscle and bone.

Cynthia's ardor is for drink and men.
A lover more dear than any other,
grade-A ex spent his money to pull
her back from riptide drugs. Undercurrents
pulled her down, alone, to set up home
on grimy streets. In a grocery cart
she pushed beer cans, clothes, a sleeping bag.

Her detoxification complete, Carlos, sweet
old ex, joined her to live on the street,
until a heart attack close to the West End
finished him off. The dead papa turtle dove
still alights in memory.

Jerry, faithful substitute now,
sleeps with her beneath the bottlebrush tree.
He'll take her back anytime
when Mario's whiskey eyes scare her away
with flashing threats of jealous blows.
Her delicate, dragonfly-beauty gone,
her makeup for years has been surplus dirt
from Santa Monica's streets
and rivulets on her cheeks.

The voice Jerry hears at dusk
was heard inside a suburban home.
That valentine voice, hardened,
has pierced at least three hearts.
There was, there is, that sparkling core
beneath the witty words that fly.

❧ YOUR CHOICE

"Cynthia, two men compete for your charms,
somewhat tarnished—pardon me—though they be.
Each wants to be your love for keeps.
Tell me, who will you choose? Your choice,
how bad will it be? You know my point of view."

Her beauty, in pre-drug days
like an English garden,
is pictured now in disarray,
a photo dropped to the sidewalk,
and stepped on many times.

"I really care for Mario
with bloody feet.
He walks painfully slow, drunk,
in boots that do not fit.
Jerry's such a nice man.
He always wants me back.
He works one day a week
in a vegetable stand.
But he has no fire, nor force,
no snap, no sparkle!"

Jerry sits by the Post Office, cast on his leg,
Cynthia's resigned friend, sidewalk
proto-saint, waiting out pauses
between Mario's drunken blows
that mark her face
with a wild persistent lover's
personal brand.

❧ GROCERY-CART GOURMET MEALS

His broken left leg healed, but poorly aligned,
Jerry limps through displays of vegetables and fruits,
close to one-thirty, closing time, on outdoor market day.
He makes his way, stand to stand,
while Cynthia follows, acknowledging
peddling produce is his area of semi-expertise.

He helps others by asking farmers,
"Give what you can for making meals
for people in need." His goal:
two grocery carts of vegetables and fruit.

He and Cynthia, quixotic pair,
take donations to Rachelle's apartment,
where she, with wand-like skill,
prepares pans of creative stir-fry,
pots of zappy soup and vegetable stew.
Wouldn't you like to taste her red onion
and red potato special for today?
Fruit, whole or in halves, complete
the gourmet meals two tattered people
and a grandmother addicted to compassion,
street waiters, serve from grocery carts,
rusted and creaking, afternoon waning,
there where temporary stands have disappeared.

"Hey, this is a lot better than baloney sandwiches
or meatloaf or hash or the mystery meal
served at Ocean Park Community Center every day!"

❧ ONION SKINS

Peel them back to get the sense...

The Old Testament, bountiful well...
give alms as offerings of praise.
Add a smiling face to all your gifts

and be cheerful for a while.
Share your beer and odd loneliness.
Yahweh rewards ten times over.

Ron has no distinctive qualities,
until you peel back onion skins.
He has retirement income, a nice apartment.

Most nights, Jerry and Cynthia, "friends,"
sleep on their mattress in the Camp
under stars, back of the West End.

When heavy rains come, Ron offers a bed
and, from time to time, beer and talk...
"Do not sound a trumpet."

He protects privacy, keeps watch
unrelentingly over personal things,
does not run a charity house,

does not keep community
more than an hour or two.
Then he wants to be alone to read,

to read *Tobit* and to write on a yellow pad,
"never turn your face from any poor man,
and that includes women, too."

❧ ANTONIO

Close to the Post Office where mail trucks come and go,
Cynthia sits against the NO PARKING post. I stop to talk.
It's been a while, she says, since she saw me around.
She wants me to know about Antonio.

"A week ago I found him dead,
early, when I went for water
across the street from the West End,
where they go for fun, but we don't.
You need money to dance and drink.
I found him kneeling, both hands cold,
clutching the metal fence, like steel.
His penis showed. Pathetic old man!
Must have been trying to pee."

Cynthia gathers grime like a backyard barbecue.

"I ran to the Camp to yell, *Antonio's dead!*
They came alive back of the West End,
where we sleep, Jerry, Shane and I.
At night we watch stars. They watch us.
They seem to know in their glowing way
we are too tired for transforming luck."

Cynthia puts both hands into the air
as if trying to touch those stars, then
brings her arms around, lacing her fingers,
as if embracing her old phantom friend.

"Antonio's been here thirty years.
Dumpster hopping was his work.
He shared food and talk with us
but slept alone on the other side.
He once told me he prayed a lot.
We'll miss those weary eyes."

I walk away carrying Cynthia's sadness
like a bag of oranges about to spill.
We'll tell Antonio's story a while,
then no one, no one, will ever tell it again.

DUMPSTER DIVER

All day long into garbage bins
for collectibles and clothes, Mike,
a dumpster diver, dives.

He likes the freedom of his work,
discovery, even the dismay when
sadness surfaces in the letter

a child wrote to her mother who had left,
a man's unshaven face in a picture frame,
the gewgaws and forgotten baubles
that decorated pretty girls of yesterday.

Mike trades these things and sells them
five minutes from the sea, twenty-nine, once
schooled in Special Ed, his life
spindrift, now playing out, he sleeps

in the Arizona Avenue transitory kingdom Camp
close to Cynthia and Jerry, humble monarchs
who rule the cleanup, arranging
all worldly possessions behind the bar.
They keep the verbal contract
and together dream

they are at the sand, laughing, Mike diving down,
holding a fist-full ball of wet sand,
ready to throw at WC Field's illuminated
red nose, fairground stands rising from under water,
prizes floating up for pretty girls and handsome boys....

❧ GLOBAL CONNECTIONS

I love the history of towns,
organic growth nourished
by surrounding land:
river towns, mountain towns,
farm towns...way stations
and trading posts becoming towns.

I am eager to know kinship links
for this Santa Monica farmers market,
where for thirty years I have observed
interchange between farm vendors,
shoppers and homeless poor.

In fifteenth-century Germany
three thousand towns were relay points,
each one a market place. And then came big
covered markets and bazaars, stalls groaning
with fruit, meat and game. Buy our asparagus!
Baked apples! Seville, London, Hanoi, Leipzig,
Canton, Genoa. Chickens! Ducks! Fish!

I ask student-friends to make me a globe,
a digitalized globe where lights glow,
red ones for every market town,
blue for outdoor markets found in cities
and yellow for those located in the countryside.

Behind each light, a cylinder, computerized,
provides the story about farmers
and people who make meals from produce
brought in from fields. Each town
a meeting place, each market a throbbing heart.
No such energy surges in supermarkets today.

The poor gather at markets, for they know
that people with money, ready to buy, have money to give.

❧ NOT A SAINT MARTIN OF TOURS

I am neither a Saint Martin of Tours
nor a Dorothy Day, ready to give
half or more than half of all I have away.
Still, the Parable of the Good Samaritan
survives inside me. I know
the homeless are hurt by life,
somewhat like it is for you and me,
ordinary, but surely more.

I often talk with homeless poor...friends
I call them... on this Santa Monica street.
Their feelings mirror ours in response
to arcane happenings and humdrum things—
bits for biographies no one will write.

At the near limits of familiarity,
I seek a word, to be precise, for more
than likeable folk, not confidants,
a list, concern-bound, expandable.

For now
the well-worn word *friends*
serves to classify the homeless
who have taught me about resiliency,
candor, bare-knuckle grit.

❧ RHYTHMIC FLOW

In cadences
of William Butler Yeats
they are lost, homeless,
and can't be there
with birds on golden boughs
in Byzantium, sung

as he sang
about beauty,
pangs of passing,
growing old too soon,
imperial duty, his
measured tongue
one of the great ones.

How do we inflect with accuracy—
choice and chance mixed
in smelly bodies—those who live
in broken motion?
Jimmy and Lea,

a wedded pair, neither an air
nor a zest for higher culture—
he's a drywall man, no work—

      a self with a self,
      their home this street,

 divined in a simple request:

"Give us hamburgers here
and a beer to share."

That'll do for noonday solace.

❧ REALITY

I'd like to write poetry as sublime
as Fra Angelico's frescoes
or the radiant cathedral windows in León,
as clever as Paul Klee's *The Twittering Machine*
or as confidentially sensuous
as David Hockney's sketch *Clean Boy*.
I'd even like to choose between bents for letting
words pour out in wild spitting torrents,
enigmatic sparsity or thick profound opacity.
But I can't. My brain won't cooperate, and so

I write poems about Nameless, Cynthia, Bo-J, James,
and others I have met who have done their best to sleep
without comfort of home. Maybe I'll work on a central
processing unit to keep track of why so many of them,
countrywide, end up bedded down
on mattresses of newspaper and cardboard.
I suspect not even a high-tech system
could come close to laying out the picture.

❧ FLOWER SPIKE STAMENS

At Fifth and Arizona the flower spike
stamens fall red on the sleeping pair.
Jerry could weep with the leafy shoots,
and his morning eyes are papery bark
when he goes to find beer for his love.
She says, "We're friends, but not a pair.
We've been together, I think, five years."

The West End promises a funky good time.
They've never been inside to drink
or dance or kiss. They know the mess
they've made of their lives behind.
They sleep in starts under the bottlebrush,
while Scotty Boy spins all the hits.

*

Eight years have passed, and the West End,
an empty place, no longer
attracts seekers of fun.
Cynthia, longtime lover of beer,
has gone to Florida with another man,
leaving three most dear behind:
Carlos (dead these many years),
Jerry, looks like a chimney sweep,
limps, unpacking vegetable crates
for owners of stands, when he can,
and Mario, whose severe liver disease
has cured the wildness she fearfully loved
in frenzies of alcoholic highs, before lows
bent him like a tree hit by a hurricane.

Chances are, I'll never speak to Cynthia again,
and no chance ever to see three of her four men.

Jerry, however, is apt to tap me
on the shoulder, as he has done
in scattered times, and we might wonder
about the end of her unraveling story.

❧ OFTENTIMES

Jerry sits, as he has before,
cross-legged on the sidewalk.

"In my hands I feel my father's hands
     handling summer fruit.
In my legs I feel his tired ones at four
     getting out of bed.
He does not feel my yearning to sell
     apricots again,
did not feel my sadness
     when I had to sell the truck.

"He does not feel my body asleep
     by his absence,
does not relish the salt taste
     of beady skin,
and does not smell the sweetness
     of vegetable-vendors' sweat.

"We do not drive, just at dawn,
     from Central Market.
When he died, I tried to drive the truck
     the way he did.
I could not speak as kindly to housewives
     rummaging my fruit,
could not feel his fingers grip the pen
     to keep the records straight.

"What he earned by work I spent for fun,
     and fun was nothing much.
Many mornings I slept late. He never did,
     and when my mother,
the good woman of the gospel, went,
     my desire went, too,
and now I sleep outdoors at night, and sometimes
     unpack crates at market stands."

❧ HOMELESS FRIENDS

or at least, people
worthy of concern
1675/ 2008

Marks of their individual grace amaze me.

Certain slants of urban light
brighten their faces
tired in a prosperous century,
traces of innocence and remorse
under eyebrows,
their bodies rank with scents
of who they are.

I admire the way most cope,
starting each morning, sober face,
ready to stitch together
parts of the day ahead,

as did Murillo's *Young Boys Playing Dice*
on a stone step in Seville, a step that could not
help them rise above ragged clothes,
naked shoulders. The haunted face
of the youngest—he munches crusted bread,
watching older boys concentrate on chance
flung from their fingers, hoping to win, seriously.

T JOINTS AND BUTTERFLIES

❧ EAKINS ON ARIZONA AVENUE

Although time has idealized the man,
his paintings remain a constant truth,
portraying the American people and their
world with remarkable fidelity and sympathy.
—William Innes Homer

Thomas Eakins pursued a realism so intense it transformed itself
into arias and skull competitions of poetic illusion.

The *Concert Singer* loses herself in song
far more beautiful than wistful she.
The *Cello Player* feels the belly and ribs
     of the mellow body
between his knees, dear and familiar
       as the one for whom
       he wears the wedding ring.

The Biglin brothers, in skull competition,
turn the stake, and, in my mind, leave
their elegant pod skimming water
to turn into penniless men
       on this street
almost a century and a half
after they rowed and wore
       blue bandanas on their heads.

Eakin's father *The Writing Master*, eighteen-eighty-two
and two thousand and eight, is here, intent, as usual,
to do the job of writing far better than well done.

I would like Eakins to do portraits of our homeless people,
capturing sunlight's flickering degrees of warmth
on singular faces as carefully as he painted
his father's hands in full illumination, the man
inscribing an official document on vellum.

❧ T JOINTS, FULL AND HALF-LAP ONES

Despite a neurological condition,
leaching strength from arms and hands,
James' glimmering smile and earnest voice
make a graduate of Pius the Tenth High School
and Cal State Long Beach, psychology major, winnable.

"Once you are homeless on the street, barriers are everywhere.
Every step you take to leave, obstacles push their weight against you.
The same chains of events, attitudes, fuzzy choices that brought you here
can keep you here indefinitely. It's tougher than a running back
going against an all-pro defensive line and wild-boar linebackers.
A person thrives or mires in habits, sleeping in entranceways,
like First Church of Christ Scientist or Wells Fargo Bank.
Get used to nighttime community or avoid it."

James communicates partly
with diminished body gestures,
his thought-burdened head moving
on a slow, low-range swivel

"Eruptions in small routines can force a move away from security.
Love, illness, arguments can push a person out, to move on, somewhere.
Then there is customary confusion. What factors brought me here?
I'm not so great at solving ego-construction puzzles. Later,
to put myself firmly together again, given a basic structure
already in place, storm-damaged…and for life, perhaps, in disrepair,
when I'm composed, since I do know the finer arts of carpentry—
learned in part-time work—I could on a good day,
manipulate T joints, full and half-lap ones, dado joints
dovetail variations, crisscross joints and double laps."

&❧ WISDOM OF CHANCE

"I thought my way was up, all the way.
No Heraclitean down for me.
The wisdom of chance puzzles me.
Is chance enough alive to be wise?

"It may be that an undernourished brain
causes me to be classified as nervous type."

      "Well, James, to some degree we all belong
      in the nervous class, heading up and down,
      watching the ways up and down merge."

James has a degree in psychology,
      "for understanding me."

"Lot's of things are curious,
like why I'm black and not wearing shoes.
Why I'm on the job with a begging cup.
Should I dress for the occasion?"

His arms listless, fallen, and a paper cup
      in front of his feet,
James has a nineteen-forty's-film quiet smile
      and body language to signify,

"Depression got a headlock on me
and caused a neurological disorder
or, probably, the other way around.
Took all the strength out of my arms,
my hands, and most of what matters to me.

"I had no intention to be
a hapless inhabitant on this street.
You don't think I think about
attaining peak experiences, my feet

solidly planted, to survey reality?
On the day-by-day practical plane,
I'd like to hold down a job
and eat some pasta
with culturally informed friends."

❧ UNCANNY SPIDER

James doesn't speak with arms and hands,
       not even with eyes.
       It's his voice, a second violin.

"You may want to know why I have
so little hope… and, with my intelligence.
I wanted to be a counselor or adolescent psychologist
to understand myself and others odd like me.
A neurological disorder defeated my strategies.
I am the kid continuously strange.

"Like a colony of ants my momentary selves
are out collecting bits of information.
I am a spider trying to catch everything
in a vast web of understanding.
My family can't fathom me at all,
and that puts me in free fall, landing here,
the reluctant panhandler, out of synch all the time.
You know, in college, my departmental advisor cautioned me
about my uncanny interest in theories of personal identity.
Sometimes sentences are so intense they appear
as if burned by a woodburning set's hot needle
onto a panel in my brain.

"*A community is a network of social relations
marked by mutuality and emotional bonds.*
I belong to several. They don't acknowledge I exist.
In art appreciation class, I tried to become a tree,
adjusting to Ruskin's first law for them, express beauty
in tapering. Spring up and reach out. I didn't follow
the Law of Graceful Diminution: let your ego diminish
in exact proportion to the size of the branches your trunk sends out.

"*Such a conglomeration of characters makes up a fantastic,
ageless bestiary.* I remember sentences and film images
the way a fanatic recalls all the great sports events.

La dolce vita. Instead of the sweet life, it's the street, *La strada,* where some of the animal silhouettes barely hold precious sparks of human life. Were he alive, Fellini could capture us on film, helping us to see our mix of misery and mystery, both collecting at the core of Keirsey and Bates' *Please Understand Me."*

❧ BO J

I

Last night Bo J slept in shadow
down by the court house
on Santa Monica's subdominant side.

Bo J doesn't want indoor jobs.
He'd rather be with a work gang, to sing.
No, not with a work gang,
but on the street, to sing
songs bluer than blue
in homeless tempo, wandering beat.

All day long they work so hard.
Bo J never works for a paycheck wage.
Sam Cooke sings from his whole body,
my work is so hard..."

Guitar and voice together beget
          truer blues, regal ones,
blowing spirit's breath
way up and down with seventh chords,
          clapping gospel hymns
and songs black men used to sing
to do the work they had to do.

Bo J, near the Abysinnian Baptist Church,
Harlem afternoons, learned to play the strings,
and struggled with fear when it got dark.

A daylight master
of cool unstable intonation,
his concert halls are well-walked streets,
till the sun is going down
working on the highway and byways...

Bo J takes me there to hear
songs people sing, right here,
working on the chain gang,
singing, working so hard
until Evening starts whispering
to its confrere Imminent Night,
          "Come quick."

                    II

Bo J is back,
guitar and repertoire,
terra cotta face. A drooping mustache
and humorous lower lip's upward curve
            create an ellipse.
I've missed the rhythm of his tenor blues.

"Where you been on market day, my friend?"

      "I been sick."

      "I heard you were in jail."

"Oh that don't mean much. I been to Wayside.
You collect points for doing little things:
no permit to sing a song on the edge of the crowd,
or borrowing some big store's grocery cart,
or opening a bottle when not inside to take a sip.
Five points earned me a vacation with restraints."

"It's good to have you back to sing.
We need a reason on days like this
to slow our hurrying down the street."

"Thank you, sir. Thank you very much.
It's nice the way you call me back.
I've been longing… so long…
to belong here. What kind of song?
Man and woman trouble?
What kind of song you want today?"

"Oh, just sing your soul, Bo J.
Sing it free, and very sad…
funny, too, some, if you want.
I'm waiting to hear,"

You know fire makes me hot
and ice keeps 'em cold
but I need a whole lot of woman
to satisfy my soul.

III

Bo J's not feeling well today.

"Must be somethin' catchin' in the air."

Dreadlocks fall from under his hat.
He seems too weak to sing the blues.

A fake-leather coat
and street-weathered guitar
look as sad as his mottled face,
awash today with weariness.

"Sing me a song?"

"Ain't got no choice."

He's a sidewalk artist doling out.
Ain't no sunshine when she's away.
The pink pick moves across the strings.
Bo J's on stage. Here to perform.

"You make me feel good anytime."

"That's kind of you to say those words."

Ain't no sunshine when she's gone
and she's always gone, too long
anytime she's gone away.

❧ PSYCHOLOGY OF ADJUSTMENT

proposed by James

Hey, Bo J, once you're here on the street, you know,
you're lucky to get off. So let's compensate for accommodations
that are, frankly, somewhat bleak. We could, through imagination,
transform our living space into a center for learning skills
to help us change crud and spit into murals and manic poetry,
using aerosol cans to paint facades like flamboyant macaws
(red, yellow, blue, black and white), plus graffiti collages.
We can take a fling, too, at conceptual art, using words
found on discarded cardboard boxes and flyers:

> WE PEE LIKE YOU
> AND HAVE FEELINGS TOO.

Or, hell, how about setting up pavilions subsidized by benefactors,
pennants flying freely in sea-spawned fog, entrance fee nothing,
ring-toss, dart games, spin-the-wheel wildly, bringing kids
to eat pink and blue cotton candy, signing up itinerant musicians
to play progressive jazz, rock 'n roll, Tennessee hillbilly music,
and, yes, even string quartets and Bach cantatas?
When it rains, let stars fall like fireflies out of the sky,
while we sleep half-awake, seaside, on towels of every damn color
found in a crayon box, protected by gigantic beach umbrellas,
listening all night to the unending Pacific symphony.

❧ FRACTURED SYNTAX

E. E. Cummings knew that absence
doesn't shut off presence,
anyone's, so I don't hesitate
to ask him in sun, wind and rain
to help me write about forgotten
who-knows-for-sure-wheres,
here homeless on Arizona Avenue,
where post-traumatic recall often fails,

so Cummings and his dad, singing each leaf,
keep us moving through dooms of love,
haves of give, days and nights
of keep in mind to help Mario
try not to take another sip, because
the clinic's dire liver report says
almost time to depart, and so, I guess

fractured syntax is just fine
when stars of concern—due regard—
like manna falling, glow, shoppers
and visitors welcome anytime,
if they share money,

so, watch Cynthia in her wheelchair
at her post on the street, a scream
hanging out with foul-mouthed,
laughing men, make speed races
on flying wheels past stone benches
at the Post Office to get there where,
just on time, at the public restroom, and,

you know, Jerry has diabetes bad, works
when he can at a produce stand, waits for an apartment,
a subsidized loss of freedom he says, while Mario

rages with gnomic outbursts, at odds with the kind
Cummings might offer lovingly about people,
none that far from the end.

❧ DREADLOCKS MYSTICALLY

Lewis with milk-chocolate dreadlocks
talks of growing-up marvels and mysteries
begun in Silver Springs, where he found
himself on August mornings hot at play.

"I lived outside, still do.
In Maryland I first felt lust.
Still do. But I have vowed
to sublimate. Hey, sublimate!"

His voice, rich in nuance like that of a Shakespearean actor
reciting Lear's "houseless heads and unfed sides," blazes,

"Hobbler that I be beyond dead-end streets,
I found this knobby stick for walking,
part of a tree, hardened, gnarled, looks
like a cross, on Santa Barbara's beach."
He raises it high above his head,
poverty's heraldic device.

"Some day I hope to be a better me
in Silver Springs again, happily,
to sing in the choir, ready to shake
dreadlocks mystically, ready
for a wash in cleansing waters,
clean to the bone, glistening,
like Sunday morning clothes
when I was young and virginal!"

❧ SLEEPING ARRANGEMENTS

I have known numerous homeless:
here for a while, most move on.
If you talk about them,
Tell it right or tell it not.

Just find an overhang,
a space for crawling in,
a doorway to an establishment
where somebody says, "Okay."

Pulled each day by necessity's
gravitation, each lodger
seeks a place for night-long rest,
before getting on the next day.

Like boy scouts on a weekend trip,
many sleep in the open air.
A few have a bed inside somewhere,
but many roll up in a sleeping bag.

Billy D is not a pleasant person.
"Life sucks," is his appraisal.
"You ask where I sleep at night?
Right here, in my godamned wheelchair."

He leans back rigidly defiant,
speaks his mind, keeps
direct eye contact, beyond deception,
no frills of customary propriety.

"Right here on this stinking sidewalk.
Nobody takes care of me.
An extra buck would be a sign
of your genuine concern."

❧ TWO EDWARDS

I

I've met two homeless Edwards on this street.
I can, for all concerned, call them
Edward the First and Edward the Second.
Or let them be Afro- and Anglo-Edwards for me.
Both affirm gladly a birth-certificate's first name.
Don't shorten it or make it breezy to make it easy.
Each name declares that irrepressible self *I'm Me,*
Edward, glad to be a special person, significantly.

Thinking that I, too, can be victim, poor,
a stranger suddenly in a strange place, alone,
my aim is to treat everyone with respect.

That's how Edward treated me. He didn't impose
himself unduly, asking for "a bit of change."
I was the one to push on with a question.
"What brings you here to live on the street,
holding out your hand, requesting help?"

"It's a matter of honor, sir.
You seem to know honor.
It's a dishonorable time.
Honor your parents, your enemies,
your friends. Honor all who leave dishonorable ways.
I worked faithfully, sir, honorably, until two years ago.
Then they dishonored me with racial slurs,
saying I lacked their cooperative approach.
I'm guilty of a lot of things. No pride in that.
But I will not dishonor Lady Honor, sir, my queen.
Even in my circumstances, I look her in the eye."

II

Edward sits away, Arizona and Sixth,
from midday rain, immobile, faint, alone.
His body forms an upside-down bent Y.
His legs in the doorway spread out in a V,
upside down, too, to my eyes looking down.

"The library's a warmer place for an hour."

    "Too many eyes," he says.
    "They see thoughts flying in my head."

An Egyptian cross on a chain
decorates his chest,
a lady's gift for engagement.

"Inside, my real cross afire,
pain from many kinds of fear,
presses my heart wherever I am.
It's been this way since I was a kid.

"Waiting, I just sit here. No sense of time.
I watch the sparrows, secure in flocks.

"My good-people parents, loving me, breathed,
and wanted me to breathe, Salvation Army faith.
For more than forty years I faded in their home.
When Mother died, I couldn't do my work.

"The Lady of the Egyptian Cross
offered her home, I don't know why,
until in her wild bed I imitated death.
She said my illness frightened her.

"I want to put an end to my need to smoke
before they open my throat to help me breathe,
before they lay me out naked in the morgue,
naked to strangers' eyes
and strange to the eyes of God."

❧ STRAW BLONDE

Loud as a crow's caw on your lawn:

"A ramblin, gamblin woman,
that's what I am," sings Faye,
"Arizona Avenue, Santa Monica,
capital C, capital A." Faye's songs,
three-note range, duplicate her hurt
lingering on.

"Once I was a high school girl.
Peroxide blond. Long black socks.
Scandalous skirt. Cigarettes.
Looks like a prostitute, superiority said"

Every song's a chant, same tune.
"My walkin' man walked right away,
to Heaven's gates, they seem to say.
I've looked in alleys for his face.
God holds back too much of his grace."

New style for the street:
three-dollar wig, straw blond,
bought on a loan, held in place
on her clip-clip shaven head
by deep black viscid hair-bond glue.

"I've got nerves too high on pain."

Sidewalk chair...
"A happy child, that's what I was.
At twenty-two the breakdown came.
Mom and Dad tried for years
to bring me back from crazy ways.
In wrinkled photos they grew old."

No one else can sing her songs,
hers alone, heart
like a dropped cantaloupe
split open.

❧ TANÍA: YEAR OF SORROW

Tanía says she's Cherokee.
Her saying this conjures up
perpetrated pages of awful history.
Her people were there where Georgia,
Tennessee and North Carolina touch
in the Great Smoky Mountains.

Church, school, farms,
grist mills, blacksmith shops, plow,
spinning wheels, sawmills and looms
were stars of civilized life.

In eighteen-thirty-eight, year of sorrow,
the Removal Acts forced them to tread
on protesting feet one thousand miles west
beyond the distant *Father of Waters*
into the territory of Oklahoma, unkind.
The trail of tears for Sequoya's people
made letters of his syllabary
turn foot-wounds-bleeding red.
Thousands died walking to the Plains.
Hostile tribes intensified consternation.

The police won't let her
settle down in the outdoor market.
They know she's here for money,
and that's uncomfortable for many.
Her tanned, bare arms bear tattoos
of bucking horses at the rodeo.

"My home state? New Mexico.
My dad, a broken Cherokee
raised in Tierras, lived in Albuquerque
with my alcoholic mom and me.
I loved them both hopelessly to the bone.

Here on this street, home to the homeless,
they call me *Baby Girl*. I guess I am."

❧ JOSHUA AT SIXTY-FIVE...

war vet, fair health,
marginally employable...

"When my wife knew she had to go,
she said her wish was to fade away
there where, happily, she grew up...
ashes sent to the sea."

I took my grandson, eleven-years old,
to meet Joshua, who painted black butterflies
and flowers with green petals and purple leaves
and sold his cardboard-matted paintings
for twenty-five dollars apiece,

Joshua came back broke, unbelieving, to Santa Monica...
lived here as a child...alcoholic parents...wanted
to be near the Salvation Army Store, where believers
nurtured a neglected kid's desire to play in a band.

"And so we sold the photography shop
and drove away from Phoenix forever,
money at hand for an indefinite stretch—
we hoped—in Santa Barbara, seaside."

I wanted my Nick
to talk to this man
who temporarily slept
in the doorway of a store,
permission given, and who
gave priceless coins of concern
and shares of his small savings
to the street's most hurt,
most vulnerable, women especially,
before he went, a civilian hire,
to Iraq.

❧ OUTDOOR MARKET

"Sample our apples! Taste our berries! Organic!"
Market day, Santa Monica. People come:
matrons, lovers, select restaurateurs,
tourists, state inspectors, writers, retired fathers.
They come for fruit, flowers, veggies.
Young mothers, too, in pairs,
push their strollers, tasting strawberries,
speaking Russian, Canadian French, Spanish,
Vietnamese, homebred English.

Edith Pearl says she's from Missouri.
"Goin' back next week." Needs money.
She's been repeating this declaratively
more than a panhandling year.
Her husband is a ready roofer.
"Lots of work back there
for legal residents, like we are.
Don't stare, please, at my ugly gums."

Red potatoes, zucchini, lettuce,
raddicchio, endive, oranges, brown eggs
fill carts people push and pull. Organic forms
and their names pile in sculptural semblance,
like Raushenberg's *L.A. Uncovered # 12, 1998*,
vermillion and blue tower of city scenes,
a photo shop, its door a door to other doors,
a display window telling stories in frames.
Assemblages for today. Solicitors cry,
"Please, one dollar for battered women and kids."

As a teenager wild about Earl Scruggs,
Harlan learned picken' on the ole banjo.
He was the middle one of five kids
who wouldn't farm their lives away:

"Once you're here for a year or two
no one believes you had intentions
to be reliable, the steady, family sort.
Cracks and flaws have had their way.
Looks like I'm on the street to stay."

NOWHERE'S NOWHERE

❧ INSALATA FRUTTI DI MARE

Hundreds of feet keep walking by.
Nameless, reclusive as a cloistered nun,
does not talk unless enticed
by carefully framed
communication plans, then,
voice soft, diction clear,
she phrases her thought
in let-me-be-exact, evasive style.

"What kind of work did you once do?"

"I was not a bureaucratic part."

"You ever work for someone else?"

"Questionnaires are not for me."

"Given a wish, what would you do?"

"I'd cook salsa di noci with fettuccine,
tomatoes and walnuts, promiscuously,
the way my mother taught me to do."

"You'd cook Italian, your mother's style?"

"I'd play with tortellini and linguine
and stuffed ground veal in cannelloni.
I'd serve peccorino from goat's milk
with insalata frutti di mare prepared
with no one's encouraging kiss."

She sits on her milk crate,
ponderously, near the Pacific,
letting her self-made sign,
silently ask for subsistence pay.

"What did you eat for lunch today?"

"Something slightly better than hay."

NAMELESS

Mounted with sapphire sea and diamond sky,
Santa Monica is an affluent jewel of a city.
Nameless, heavy lady, sits on a milk-crate.
Her back rubs the wall of Promenade Footwear,
while she grows cold and wet in winter rain.
Without speaking words, she solicits help.
Doesn't raise her eyes. Sits on the street
and watches feet hurriedly pass.
A cardboard sign is her entreaty:
HOMELESS AND BROKE
AND THAT'S NO JOKE.

Ask her name, she hasn't one.
"Call me Nameless—not saying this for fun.
Names are for people with homes.
If I had one, with swooping flourishes
I'd sign checks, my name printed
in the upper left-hand corner."

Nameless speaks Brooklynese,
her half-smile wrought senile
by broken-blackish decayed teeth.
"I come from nowhere's nowhere.
Truth is I don't have a future either.
The more questions you ask,
the more I'll try to shut my mouth.
Like swallows, I should have gone south,
maybe to an isolated island
where people don't enjoy the sound
of wise voices coming from puffed-up
chests and breasts."

❧ JAGUAR LADY

A Jaguar XJ6 pulls in and parks...

Arizona Avenue, a block south of Wilshire's
Miracle Mile going east, hums twice a week
on outdoor market day. Strategically, Nameless
works this street for a bite to eat,
works by letting her weight

spread out while seated on a milk-crate,
showing the petition-sign
to declare her situation here today: broke.

Across the sidewalk from Nameless—that's the name
she answers to—a lady descends,
glowing in black leather from toe
to quivering throat, and does not pause,
offers no boon.

Nameless, with her almost formless body, looks down.

❧ TOUCH OF CLASS

A quick, shy smile passed away.
"I'm from The East, and I am lost.
But better times will come at last."

Against a wall Nameless
sat massive, unbearably still,
eyes closed, letting her sign
relate her needs: broke, no joke.

She would not engage with eyes or talk
until my words, discretely aimed,
asked her name, her place for growing up.

In composed response
she measured each word,

"If I had a home, I'd have a name
and a spacious room with an angel's bed
to bless my legs, comfort my head
the same soft way night after night.
I'd never fret here on the street,
soliciting with lesser nighthawk wit
and dark glasses favoring eyes
that hurt in reflected light."

Nameless is homeless with a style
born of what nurturing, who can guess.

"No name," she said, "and where I'm from
means not a bit to people like you.
You want to know my fall from grace."

❧ VERBATIM

The wind blows cold from the sea,
a bit of Wednesday Pacific misery
for outdoor marketers, and for Nameless
who sleeps at night, a huge cat curled against the wall
that separates Wells Fargo Bank from Arizona Avenue,
near preferred shops on the Third Street Mall,
where younger generation activity goes till late;

but Nameless now, in beanbag purple pants,
wearing a black sweater over sundry layers of clothes,
wearing half-hose on crusted legs, has her fish-net scarf
and her orange snood encircled by a Tintoretto halo,
head bowed, during this break in intermittent rain.

"Italian still?" I question, soft mockingly.

　　　"Pure tortellini true." She looks up.
　　　"Two immigrant cells with pasta secca
　　　stirred with virgin olive oil."

"Any brothers or sisters write to you?"

　　　"I might get into that someday
　　　when you are far enough away."

"Made any friends in this street community?"

　　　"No time for that. Think what it costs in care
　　　to have a friend who lasts for years.

　　　"You think you have a right, self-assigned,
　　　to bring my private life within your sight."

❧ AS IMAGINED POET

"I had an education once."

At the outdoor market in light rain
she sits on a milk-crate chair.
If she had the will, which she doesn't,
she could write a makeshift poem.

"No nightingale merits an ode
when I can't have scrumptious food.
Let me praise the gawky crow
or flocks of silly cement sparrows.
Don't think I'd hesitate to write loftily
about stale urine smells that invade
my doorway dreams at night
when sleeping bags put out the lights.

"I had an Italian mother, too near
to bear a daughter's rebellious times,
and a foul-mouthed vanishing father
whose hairy arms I still hold dear.
I could praise them in lyrical words,
sincere to a point, or I could write an ode
about sick flies that covet morsels
that are mine by divine right
of homeless misery.

"To be honest,
I'd like a resurrected life, no broken teeth,
no swollen legs, no shame. On this curb
I could sing...a sidewalk singer...
in twilight eternity... maybe an actor...
this street a familiar stage... or a poet...
no...a singer singing *Dear Old Pal of Mine*,
bel canto style!"

❧ MIST

A solitary seagull, limping a bit,
bites at a piece of sidewalk bread
where Nameless, absent now, should sit
on her milk-crate, waiting for coin,
her legs crusted, begging,
swollen feet, ready wit, she could not
do the two-step here, big body
clad like a clown, her space
zero against the wall.

I push a bill deep enough to fall away
in pocket time, to wait....
I do not speak.

A dozen gull-mates with kee-yah voices
join in to snatch up bread.
They leave the limping seagull none.
Nameless has vanished
like the morning's mist
now burned away in midday sun.

❧ CALL ME HOUSE FINCH

*Lingua Franca... a language
of inter-ethnic communication.*
—Mikael Parkvall

I don't live the way they do,
in bleached brown, grey, dingy
khaki clothes, sparrows for me alone,
the homeless, drab-hopping,
each heart beating
its customary pulse, pulse...
commutable desires under the skin

collected in hurt-proof parts,
flaring, fading, flaming up again,
whether they choose or not.

Call me house finch or canary thrush.
I've got color in my clothes.
In common lingua bird-like franca,
we converse a transitory
ictus-while, then take flight
in socially distinct ways,
to keep on flying, tired or not.

❧ BREATHING SUBSIDES

The Third Street Promenade comes down
from Wilshire, one block north of Arizona,
and ends at Broadway, two blocks south.
The young converge here weekend nights.
At bookstores people browse and buy
from mid-morning until late at night:
Borders, Arcana, Midnight Special,
Hennessey and Ingalls.
Buy something at Brookstone, Rockport,
Banana Republic, Promenade Footwear
(shoes like Kenneth Cole and Havana Joe).
Eat at the Broadway Bar and Grill,
Lago, Bravo Cucina, or a dozen other eateries.
Unsettled people spend here until spent, late,
and often wish they could stay to spend again.
It's a magnet drawing the homeless, too.
You can't sleep in the Promenade, though.
At night you must go to intersecting
Arizona, where, after a while,
breathing subsides....

ALPHABETS, END TO END

❧ KIDS WILL PLAY

Law enforcement artists project
what a child might look like years hence.
I go the other way around, wondering
what the homeless I know here,
in visits to this street, were like as kids
before emotional storms unhinged them,
before accidental happenings
unhitched them from household ways.

Paul Klee reminds us:

She Howls While We Play?

Three whelps
tumble over each other
and entwine
while the mother
yelps vexation

until at last, rest assured, they tire
and need her love for what time
she might be there to offer it.

The other side,
the dark side of anyone's life
is there in Klee's *Drummer*, an eye
within the question-mark-scythe-noose,
tightening...the exclamation mark as tie,
tightening...the universal colors of death,
red, white and black, threatening.

From childhood on
we learn to suffer
and to find fun, ultimate rhythms
for every age, and so,

in their honor, I mean the homeless,
let's play and keep at our work.

❧ FAREWELL HANDS

Small wonder that so many people
have attributed the origins
of their alphabets to their gods.
—Ben Shahn

Shahn, were he here, would be the one
to do the mural of Farewell hands
reaching up, beautifully drawn.
That's the way it is and will be
among our homeless citizens,
today unkempt, tomorrow gone.

In the calligraphic Hebrew of *Pleiades*,
full of dots and lines suggesting
molecular structures and starry spaces,
thou shalt not let tongue and lips
form unfair words about those
whose address is only a street.

When the Saints play clarinets
and trombones in five dimensions,
let those who raise their hands in *Identity*
know we remember gold-leaf constellations,
letters from the Hebrew alphabet,
and colored polygons from *Where Wast Thou?*
And if not we, then articulate prophets, saying,

No one knows, precisely, the ways the last and least
inherit golden menorahs, serigraphs
and allegorical masks, blessed by glittering stars,
when we achingly reach places to rest.

No one knows for sure how Ben Shahn,
seer of graphic arts, divined
contour lines, kaleidoscopic colors,

and deity-alphabets that, end to end, create
polychrome patterns of hope for homeless poor,
who, like us, live at the edge of light and night.

NOTES

Bouquet
I translated two lines from "Apegado a mí," the ninth lullaby from *Canciones de Cuna*. The three words Tenderness (*Ternura*), Desolation (*Desolación*) and Devastation (*Tala*) are titles of three of Mistral's four books of poetry. There are several legends in Chile that relate the origin of the copihue. One tells how some survivors of a great battle climbed trees, from which they saw their dead friends, and as they wept, their tears became flowers.

WHERE WAST THOU?
With the title of this first section I want to tie together its first poem, "Alphabets", with the book's last poem, "Farewell Hands", whose middle stanza celebrates gold-leaf constellations, the Hebrew alphabet and colored polygons that appear in Shahn's dazzling *Where Wast Thou?* This painting makes me wish I could write with gold leaf the names of the homeless I know. "Where wast thou?" I ask, and each answers, it seems, "Homeless on the street. I bear a special name and use it to sign my identity with letters from our alphabet. May my farewell hands link us forever."

Alphabets
There has to be a special connection between alphabets and names. An alphabet enables writing, and what is written stands out and endures. When children in kindergarten or first grade are learning to write the letters of the alphabet, the custom is that each first learn to write his or her own name.

Asking Favors
It seems that John Ruskin, the leading English art critic of the Victorian Age, had a morbid fear of light spots against a dark background, whether in art or nature, and this is a plausible explanation of why he denounced Rembrandt's "alarming explosions" of light. See John D. Rosenberg's *The Darkening Glass: A Portrait of Ruskin's Genius.* Consult Rembrandt's name in the index.

Hemerocallis
"Hemerocallis" is the botanical name for the daylily. This flower sleeps and blooms, sleeps and blooms. I have watched daylilies in my garden follow this sequence.

Trampled Gardens
Carlos Saura's film *Flamenco* inspired me to write this poem.

Far Away and Near at Hand
Italian neorealism was a trend in filmmaking prominent in the forties and fifties. With its democratic spirit and compassionate point of view, with its emphasis on the value of

ordinary people and its use of nonprofessional actors, even for principle roles, neorealism was an approach to filmmaking that attracted innumerable film goers. Vittorio De Sica was the director of *The Bicycle Thieves* (1948). Roberto Rossellini was the director of *Open City* (1945). Rosselini's *Paison*, which I saw while I was in college, was the film that impressed me more than any other film I saw for many years.

Give me for Starts
Brooks' petitioning sign struck me, and still strikes me, as unusual.

THE CAMP
"The camp" is a proper name, designating one particular location.

Onion Skins
In the *Book of Tobit* in the *Old Testament*, Tobit patiently accepts his blindness. His son Tobiah, accompanied by the angel Raphael, catches fish, by which his father's blindness is cured. Rembrandt's etching in the Albertina in Vienna shows the elderly Tobit groping his way toward the door, a small dog at his feet, while the fish, high in the fireplace, are drying.

Global Connections
"Daily life within a small radius was provided for by weekly or daily markets in the town…." Fernand Braudel, *The Structures of Everyday Life*, Harper & Row, p. 507. This sentence appears in a wonderful section about markets and towns worldwide in the 15th and 16th centuries. This digitalized globe is, of course, imaginary.

Wisdom of Chance
When James speaks about peak experiences, we know that he refers to Abraham Maslow's *Toward a Psychology of Being*, a book much read in the 60's and 70's. One of my former students told me this book was assigned reading in four of his classes in one semester. Maslow lays out a theory of self-actualization, which is the basis for his humanistic psychology.

Uncanny Spider
The first italicized sentence is found in Thomas Benders *Community and Social Change in America*, Johns Hopkins University Press, 1978, p. 7. The second italicized sentence is found in Gilbert Salachas's *Federico Fellini*, Crown Publishers, Inc., 1970, p. 52.

Bo J
Bo J has a special liking for Sam Cooke's songs. Cooke was an American gospel, R & B, soul and pop singer and song writer. He had 29 top 40 hits between 1957 and 1965. On December 11, 1964 he was murdered by the motel manager, "justifiable homicide," in a motel in Los Angeles.

Fractured Syntax
Any reader of Cummings' poetry knows he uses an idiosyncratic syntax. During World War I he was confined to a concentration camp La Ferté Macé, France. Several of the

people confined with him became "Delectable Mountains." I think that the homeless I write about are also Delectable Mountains.

Outdoor Market
Robert Rauschenberg (1925-2008) was famous for his assemblages, which consist of objects found in the street and images, e.g., photographs. I think it was in 1991 that my wife Tacui and I went to the National Gallery of Art in Washington, D. C. to see an exhibit of Rauschenberg's *Overseas Cultural Exchange*. I warm to the idea of found objects becoming art.

Call Me House Finch
Lingua Franca: "The most important legacy of the language's
once dominant position in inter-ethnic communication
in the Mediterranean is of course that its name
has entered not only English, but also numerous
other languages as a generic term for precisely that—
a language of inter-ethnic communication."
       —Mikael Parkvall

With each homeless person I came to know we found a vocabulary rooted in common interests that served our needs for conversation. I can say that in each case we found a lingua franca.

Kids Will Play
Children learn early that we are all death-bound. Many children, in fact, confront death in their own families. Martin Heidegger has written profoundly in *Being and Time* how we humans are the beings bound towards death. Our consciousness-in-the-world is rooted in our awareness that we are mortal. Our sense of play and our engaging in play temper this awareness. Playing and dying always link in our minds. Cynthia and Nameless, for example, play with words, James plays with large ideas, and Bo J plays his guitar. These skills, honed in playing, are put at service of work by people who have to make a living soliciting money on the street.

Farewell Hands
"*And looking at the elegance of a page of Khmer script, at the handsome square Sanskrit, or the Arabic, at stones carved with the mysterious runes of the Anglo-Saxons, at early Greek tablets, the cuneiform stelae of the Sumerians, or at the majestic lettering on some Roman monument, who can fail to find there an immediate sense of the hand that made the letters?... Small wonder that so many people have attributed the origins of the alphabets to their gods!*" This quote is found on page 155 of Frances K. Pohl's *Ben Shahn with Ben Shahn's writings*, Pomegranate Artbooks, San Francisco, CA, 1993.

This book is set in 12 point Adobe Jenson light.

Adobe Jenson is an old style serif typeface drawn by type designer Robert Slimbach for Adobe Systems. Its roman style is based on a Venetian oldstyle text face cut by Nicolas Jenson in 1470, and its italics are based on those by Ludovico Vicentino degli Arrighi. Adobe Jenson is a highly readable typeface appropriate for large amounts of text due to its organic nature, low x-height and inconsistencies that help differentiate letters.

Nicolas Jenson was a notable 15th century printer. He studied printing for three years with Gutenberg at Mainz and was one of the first to design roman type, considered superior in beauty and alignment of characters to that of John of Speyer. Jenson started publishing under his own name and with his own type in 1470 in Venice, producing numerous celebrated editions. His roman type of 1470 furnished inspiration for Garamond, Caslon, William Morris, Bruce Rogers, and other masters. After his death, his type was used by the Aldine Press.